The Facts in the Case of M. Valdemar

Mesmerism, Mortality & the Horrifying Limits of Science

A Modern Translation
Adapted for the Contemporary Reader

Edgar Allan Poe

Translated by Tim Zengerink

Table of Contents

Preface
Message to the Reader

Rebuilding the Greatest Library in Human History

Thousands of years ago, the Library of Alexandria was the heart of global knowledge — a sanctuary where the wisdom of every known civilization was gathered and shared freely.

And then, it was lost.

Now, we're rebuilding it — and you are invited to join us.

At the Library of Alexandria, we've set out to make every book available to every person on Earth — not just in print, but in every language, every format, and for every reader.

Here's how we do it:

- **Deluxe Print Editions at True Printing Cost** - Order any book as a high-quality paperback, elegant hardcover, or stunning boxset — and only pay what it costs to print. No markups. No middlemen.
- **Unlimited Access to the Greatest Works** - Enjoy thousands of timeless classics — from Plato to Shakespeare to Tolstoy — in beautiful, modern eBook and audiobook editions. Read and listen without limits — for every reader, everywhere.
- **Modern Translations for Every Language & Dialect** - We're reimagining the classics in clear, accessible language — and translating them into every dialect imaginable. Everyone deserves to understand humanity's greatest ideas.

When you visit **LibraryofAlexandria.com**, you're not just accessing books — you're joining a global movement to restore, preserve, and share the wisdom of civilization.

Join us today at LibraryofAlexandria.com

Together, we'll ensure the light of human wisdom never fades again.

With gratitude,

The Modern Library of Alexandria Team

Visit:
www.libraryofalexandria.com
Or scan the code below:

Introduction

Poe's Exploration of Science, Death, and the Uncanny

Among Edgar Allan Poe's most unsettling and provocative works, *The Facts in the Case of M. Valdemar* (1845) stands out as a chilling blend of Gothic horror and pseudo-scientific experimentation. Unlike Poe's tales of abstract terror or supernatural forces, this story merges cutting-edge scientific curiosity with the darkest aspects of human mortality, pushing both the characters and the reader to confront the unsettling boundary between life and death. Through the medium of mesmerism—an early form of hypnotism—Poe imagines a horrifying experiment in which the dying man, M. Valdemar, is placed under a trance at the very threshold of death. What unfolds is not only a macabre narrative but also a powerful meditation on humanity's relentless quest for control over the unknown.

The story was first published in December 1845 in The American Review, and it was immediately received with shock, fascination, and even credulity. Many readers, unfamiliar with Poe's frequent blending of fiction and the scientific ideas of his time, believed the tale to be a factual report. This reaction highlights Poe's masterful use of narrative realism and scientific detail, which lend the story an unsettling authenticity. Poe, always intrigued by the interplay between rational inquiry and the inexplicable, here constructs a story that feels at once clinical and grotesque, merging the language of experimentation with the language of horror.

At its core, *The Facts in the Case of M. Valdemar* is a study of liminality—the states of being between life and death, consciousness and unconsciousness, science and superstition. The unnamed narrator, who claims to have extensive experience in mesmerism, describes his decision to attempt an unprecedented experiment: to mesmerize a man at the exact moment of death, in order to explore whether the mind can remain conscious after the body's vital functions cease. His subject, M. Valdemar, is already terminally ill with tuberculosis, and he consents to the experiment, aware that his life is nearing its end. What follows is a narrative that alternates between detached scientific observation and moments of sheer, unearthly terror.

Poe's meticulous attention to detail is one of the story's most striking qualities. The narrator records the stages of Valdemar's decline, the timing of the mesmerist passes, and the eerie responses given by the entranced man. Valdemar's voice—described as a hideous, unnatural sound coming from his body while under mesmerism—is one of the story's most memorable and terrifying images. This grotesque voice, neither fully human nor fully of this world, is a chilling embodiment of Poe's fascination with the uncanny—the unsettling space where the familiar becomes strange and horrifying. The narrator's tone, cool and clinical, only amplifies the horror by presenting these events as if they were routine scientific observations rather than the disintegration of natural law.

The climax of the story—when the mesmerized Valdemar, held in a state between life and death, is finally released from the trance and instantly collapses into a state of "liquid decay"—remains one of the most grotesque and unforgettable moments in Gothic literature. Here, Poe pushes the boundaries of both narrative form and thematic content, confronting readers with a vivid, physical representation of mortality that resists all attempts at control. The horrifying image of Valdemar's body rapidly decomposing is not only a narrative shock but also a symbolic reminder of the limits of human knowledge and the futility of trying to dominate death.

Mesmerism, Pseudo-Science, and the Victorian Obsession with the Unknown

To fully appreciate *The Facts in the Case of M. Valdemar*, it is essential to understand the cultural and scientific context in which Poe was writing. Mesmerism, named after Franz Anton Mesmer, was a widely discussed phenomenon in the 18th and 19th centuries, believed by some to involve an invisible "magnetic fluid" that could be manipulated to heal illnesses or influence consciousness. By the 1840s, mesmerism had captured the imagination of both scientists and the public, often blurring the line between legitimate inquiry and sensationalism. It was discussed in medical journals, practiced in salons, and featured in popular demonstrations, making it fertile ground for Poe's imaginative experiments.

Poe, who closely followed contemporary scientific debates, recognized the dramatic and unsettling possibilities of mesmerism as a literary device. In M. Valdemar, he exploits both the scientific and supernatural associations of the practice, suggesting that mesmerism might have the power to suspend the moment of death itself. This premise not only generates narrative suspense but also raises profound questions about the nature of life, consciousness, and the soul. Can science extend existence beyond its natural limits? What happens to the human spirit when the body is no longer alive, yet the mind remains aware? Poe uses the mesmerist experiment as a lens through which to explore these unsettling philosophical questions.

The narrator's detailed account of the experiment mimics the tone of scientific case studies of the period, lending the story a sense of credibility that made it particularly shocking to contemporary readers. Poe's blending of fact and fiction—incorporating medical terminology, clinical precision, and even the testimony of supposed witnesses—was so convincing that newspapers and magazines debated whether the story was true. This deliberate ambiguity reflects Poe's fascination with the limits of human knowledge and the tension between rationality and the unknown.

At the same time, the story critiques the hubris of scientific ambition. The narrator's willingness to conduct such a disturbing experiment on a dying man reveals the darker side of curiosity and the ethical dilemmas that arise when science oversteps its bounds. In this sense, M. Valdemar anticipates the themes of later Gothic and science-fiction works such as Mary Shelley's Frankenstein, Robert Louis Stevenson's Dr. Jekyll and Mr. Hyde, and H.G. Wells's The Island of Doctor Moreau. All of these narratives grapple with the consequences of tampering with natural laws, warning of the horrors that can result from human overreach.

The public's response to M. Valdemar also sheds light on Victorian anxieties about death and the afterlife. In an era when death was a frequent and familiar presence—due to disease, poor medical knowledge, and high mortality rates—questions about the persistence of consciousness and the possibility of an afterlife were both culturally significant and deeply personal. Poe taps into these anxieties by presenting a scenario in which death is not a clear transition but a prolonged, ambiguous state, fraught with horror and uncertainty.

Poe's Style and the Reader's Experience

Poe's mastery of tone and structure is crucial to the enduring impact of *The Facts in the Case of M. Valdemar*. The narrative unfolds as a first-person account, delivered in the voice of a narrator who insists upon the factual accuracy of his tale. This insistence on veracity, combined with the use of precise dates, times, and medical descriptions, creates an uncanny realism that draws the reader in. The narrator's matter-of-fact reporting of grotesque events—particularly the horrifying state of Valdemar's body—heightens the shock factor by presenting the unbelievable as if it were simply a matter of record.

One of Poe's most effective techniques is his ability to build tension through a slow, deliberate progression of events. The early sections of the story, which describe Valdemar's illness and the preparations for the experiment, are written in a clinical tone that contrasts sharply with the increasingly nightmarish events that follow. This shift in tone mirrors the reader's journey from curiosity to horror, making the climactic scenes all the more impactful.

Valdemar himself is a particularly haunting figure, not so much because of his personal characteristics—about which we learn little—but because of what he represents. His body becomes a battleground between life and death, a site of unnatural suspension where normal biological processes are halted by the mesmerist's will. His ghastly voice, described as coming from "the tongue and lips alone" without the usual resonance of life, is one of Poe's most chilling creations, a sound that seems to emanate from the threshold between worlds.

For modern readers, the story remains unsettling not only because of its vivid imagery but also because of its ethical implications. In an age of rapid scientific and technological advancement, Poe's cautionary tale about the dangers of crossing natural boundaries feels as relevant as ever. The idea of experimenting with the limits of life and death resonates with contemporary debates about medical ethics, artificial life support, and the definition of consciousness.

As you prepare to read *The Facts in the Case of M. Valdemar*, it is worth approaching the text not just as a horror story but as a philosophical inquiry. Poe challenges us to consider what it means to be alive, what it means to die, and whether there are boundaries that human curiosity should not cross. The story's blend of scientific precision and Gothic dread invites readers to occupy the uncomfortable space between rational thought and primal fear—a space that Poe explored more masterfully than perhaps any other writer of his time.

The Facts in the Case of M. Valdemar

Of course, I won't pretend to be surprised that the extraordinary case of M. Valdemar has sparked discussion. It would have been a miracle if it hadn't—especially given the circumstances. Because everyone involved wanted to keep the matter from the public, at least for now, or until we had more opportunities to investigate—because of our efforts to accomplish this—a distorted or exaggerated account found its way into society, and became the source of many unpleasant misrepresentations; and, quite naturally, of a great deal of disbelief.

It's now necessary for me to present the facts—as far as I understand them myself. They are, briefly, these:

For the past three years, my attention had been repeatedly drawn to the subject of Mesmerism. About nine months ago, it suddenly occurred to me that in all the experiments conducted so far, there had been a very remarkable and completely inexplicable oversight: no one had yet been mesmerized at the point of death. Several questions remained to be answered. First, whether a patient in such a condition would show any susceptibility to magnetic influence. Second, if such susceptibility existed, whether it would be weakened or strengthened by their condition. Third, to what degree, or for how long, the advance of Death might be halted by this process. There were other matters to be determined, but these questions fascinated me most—especially the last one, given the tremendously significant nature of what it might reveal.

As I searched for a suitable subject to test these specific details, I found myself considering my friend, M. Ernest Valdemar, the renowned compiler of the "Bibliotheca Forensica," and author (writing under the pen name of Issachar Marx) of the Polish translations of "Wallenstein" and "Gargantua." M. Valdemar, who had lived primarily in Harlem, N.Y., since 1839, was (or had been) especially remarkable for his extremely thin frame—his legs bearing a strong resemblance to those of John Randolph; and also for his white whiskers, which stood in stark contrast to his black hair—the latter being so commonly mistaken for a hairpiece that it became a frequent source of confusion. His disposition was distinctly nervous, making him an ideal candidate for hypnotic experimentation. On several occasions I had successfully put him into a trance with relative ease, but found myself disappointed by other outcomes that his unusual physical makeup had naturally led me to expect. His willpower was never completely or entirely under my influence, and regarding clairvoyant abilities, I could achieve nothing reliable with him. I consistently blamed my lack of success in these areas on his deteriorating physical condition. For several months before I had met him, his doctors had diagnosed him with advanced tuberculosis. He had developed the habit of discussing his impending death with remarkable composure, treating it as something that could neither be prevented nor mourned.

When these ideas first came to me, it was completely natural that I would think of M. Valdemar. I knew his calm philosophy too well to worry about any objections from him, and he had no family in America who might interfere. I spoke with him openly about the subject, and to my surprise, he seemed genuinely excited by the idea. I say this surprised me because, while he had always freely allowed me to conduct experiments on him, he had never before shown any real interest in what I was doing. His illness was the type that allowed for precise calculations about when it would end in death, and we finally agreed that he would call for me about twenty-four hours before the time his doctors predicted for his death.

It has now been more than seven months since I received the following note from M. Valdemar himself:

MY DEAR P——,

You might as well come now. D—— and F—— both agree that I won't be able to hold on past tomorrow at midnight, and I believe they've estimated the time quite accurately.

VALDEMAR

I received this note within half an hour after it was written, and fifteen minutes later I was in the dying man's room. I hadn't seen him for ten days, and I was shocked by the terrible change that this short time had brought about in him. His face had a grayish, metallic color; his eyes were completely dull and lifeless; and he had become so extremely thin that his cheekbones had broken through the skin. He was coughing up excessive amounts of fluid. His pulse could barely be felt. Despite this, he had remarkably kept both his mental clarity and some degree of physical strength. He spoke clearly—took some pain-relieving medications without help—and when I entered the room, he was busy writing notes in a small notebook with a pencil. He was sitting up in bed, supported by pillows. Doctors D—— and F—— were present.

After pressing Valdemar's hand, I pulled these doctors aside and got a detailed report about the patient's condition. His left lung had been in a semi-bone-like or cartilage-like state for eighteen months and was completely useless for sustaining life. The right lung's upper section was also partially, if not completely, turned to bone, while the lower area was simply a mass of pus-filled tubercles that had grown together. Multiple large holes had formed, and at one spot, the lung had permanently attached itself to the ribs. These changes in the right lung were relatively recent. The bone-like transformation had progressed unusually fast— no trace of it had been found a month earlier, and the attachment to the ribs had only been noticed in the past three days. Beyond the tuberculosis, the doctors suspected the patient had an aneurism of the aorta, but the bone-like symptoms made an accurate diagnosis impossible. Both physicians believed that M. Valdemar would die around midnight the following day (Sunday). It was then seven o'clock on Saturday evening.

After leaving the sick person's bedside to have a private conversation with myself, Doctors D—— and F—— had said their final goodbye to him. They hadn't planned to come back, but when I asked them to, they agreed to check on the patient around ten o'clock the following night.

After they left, I had an open conversation with M. Valdemar about his approaching death, and more specifically, about the experiment I had suggested. He continued to express his complete willingness and even eagerness to proceed with it, pressing me to begin immediately. A male and female nurse were present to care for him; however, I didn't feel entirely comfortable undertaking such a procedure with only these individuals as witnesses, should something unexpected occur. For this reason, I delayed the operation until approximately eight o'clock the following evening, when a medical student I knew, Mr. Theodore L——l, arrived and resolved my concerns. My original plan had been to wait for the physicians to arrive; but I was persuaded to move forward for two reasons: first, M. Valdemar's persistent pleas, and second, my belief that there wasn't a moment to spare, as his condition was clearly deteriorating rapidly.

Mr. L——l was kind enough to agree to my request that he record everything that happened, and most of what I'm about to tell you comes from his notes, either summarized or copied word for word.

It was about five minutes before eight o'clock when I took the patient's hand and asked him to tell Mr. L——l as clearly as possible whether he (M. Valdemar) was completely willing to let me conduct the experiment of mesmerizing him in his current condition.

He answered weakly, but clearly enough to be heard, "Yes, I want to be. I'm afraid you have mesmerized"—then immediately continued: "I'm afraid you have waited too long."

While he was speaking, I began making the hand movements that I had already discovered worked best for putting him under my influence. He was clearly affected by the first sideways stroke of my hand across his forehead; but even though I used all my abilities, no other noticeable effect occurred until several minutes after ten o'clock, when Doctors D—— and F—— arrived as scheduled. I briefly explained to them what I intended to do, and since they raised no objections, stating that the patient was already dying, I continued without delay—switching, however, from the sideways passes to downward ones, and focusing my gaze completely into the right eye of the dying man.

By this time his pulse could not be felt and his breathing was labored and noisy, occurring at intervals of half a minute.

This situation remained almost unchanged for fifteen minutes. When this time had passed, however, the dying man released a natural but very deep sigh from his chest, and the harsh, rattling breathing stopped—meaning the rough, labored sound was no longer noticeable; the pauses between breaths stayed the same. The patient's hands and feet were ice cold.

At five minutes before eleven, I noticed clear signs of the hypnotic influence taking effect. The glassy appearance in his eyes transformed into that expression of restless internal focus that only appears during sleepwalking states, and which cannot be mistaken for anything else. Using a few quick sideways hand movements, I made his eyelids flutter as they do when sleep begins, and with several more passes I closed them completely. However, I wasn't satisfied with just this result, so I continued the procedures with intensity and complete concentration of my will until I had made the sleeping person's limbs completely rigid after positioning them in what appeared to be a comfortable arrangement. His legs were stretched out fully; his arms were nearly extended as well, and rested on the bed at a reasonable distance from his torso. His head was raised just slightly.

When I finished this task, it was completely midnight, and I asked the gentlemen who were there to check M. Valdemar's condition. After conducting several tests, they confirmed he was in an exceptionally perfect state of mesmeric trance. Both doctors were extremely curious and fascinated. Dr. D—— decided immediately to stay with the patient throughout the entire night, while Dr. F—— said goodbye with a promise to come back at dawn. Mr. L——l and the nurses stayed behind.

We left Mr. Valdemar completely undisturbed until around three o'clock in the morning, when I went over to him and discovered him in exactly the same state as when Dr. F—— had left—meaning he remained in the same position; his pulse couldn't be felt; his breathing was soft (barely detectable, except when placing a mirror against his lips); his eyes were naturally closed; and his arms and legs were as stiff and cold as marble. Even so, his overall appearance was definitely not that of someone who had died.

As I moved closer to M. Valdemar, I made a partial attempt to influence his right arm to follow the movements of my own, as I gently moved my arm back and forth above his body. In previous experiments with this patient, I had never completely succeeded, and I certainly didn't expect to succeed this time; but to my amazement, his arm followed every direction I gave it with mine quite easily, though weakly. I decided to risk trying a brief conversation.

"Mr. Valdemar," I said, "are you asleep?" He didn't answer, but I noticed a slight trembling around his lips, which prompted me to ask the question over and over again. When I asked for the third time, his entire body shook with a very faint shiver; his eyelids opened just enough to reveal a thin white line of his eyeball; his lips moved slowly, and from between them, in a whisper so quiet it could barely be heard, came the words:

"Yes—sleeping now. Don't wake me! Let me die like this!"

I felt the limbs here and discovered they were just as stiff as before. The right arm, like earlier, responded to the guidance of my hand. I questioned the sleepwalker once more:

"Do you still feel pain in your chest, Mr. Valdemar?"

The response came instantly this time, though it was even quieter than before:

"No pain—I am dying."

I didn't think it was wise to disturb him any further at that moment, and nothing more was said or done until Dr. F—— arrived, who came shortly before sunrise and expressed complete amazement at finding the patient still alive. After checking the pulse and holding a mirror to the lips, he asked me to speak to the sleep-waker again. I did so, saying:

"Mr. Valdemar, are you still sleeping?"

As before, several minutes passed before he responded; during this time, the dying man appeared to be gathering his strength to speak. When I asked the question for the fourth time, he spoke very weakly, almost too quietly to hear:

"Yes; still asleep—dying."

The doctors now believed, or perhaps hoped, that Mr. Valdemar should be left alone in his current seemingly peaceful state until death arrived—and everyone agreed this would happen within just a few minutes. However, I decided to speak to him one more time, and I simply asked him the same question again.

While I was speaking, a dramatic transformation came over the face of the sleeping subject. His eyes slowly rolled open, with the pupils disappearing upward; his skin took on a deathly pallor that looked less like parchment and more like white paper; and the round, feverish red spots that had been clearly visible at the center of each cheek suddenly vanished completely. I use this description because the abruptness of their disappearance reminded me of nothing more than blowing out a candle with a single breath. At the same time, his upper lip pulled back from his teeth, which it had completely covered before; meanwhile, his lower jaw dropped with an audible snap, leaving his mouth gaping wide open and revealing his swollen and blackened tongue in full view. I assume that everyone present in the room had witnessed deathbed scenes before; but M. Valdemar's appearance at that moment was so horrifically beyond imagination that everyone instinctively stepped back from the area around the bed.

I now feel that I've reached a point in this story where every reader will be shocked into complete disbelief. It is my responsibility, however, to simply continue.

There was no longer even the slightest trace of life in M. Valdemar; and believing him to be dead, we were turning him over to the care of the nurses, when a powerful trembling movement could be seen in his tongue. This went on for about a minute. When this time had passed, there came from his swollen and still jaws a voice—one that would be insane for me to try to describe. There are, in fact, two or three words that might be thought of as partly fitting it; I could say, for instance, that the sound was rough, and fractured and empty; but the terrible entirety cannot be described, for the simple reason that no similar sounds have ever assaulted human ears. There were two features, however, which I believed then, and still believe, could reasonably be mentioned as defining qualities of the tone— as well suited to give some sense of its supernatural strangeness. First, the voice seemed to reach our ears—at least mine—from an enormous distance, or from some deep cave beneath the earth. Second, it struck me (I'm afraid, indeed, that it will be impossible to make myself understood) as sticky or slimy substances affect the sense of touch.

I have mentioned both "sound" and "voice." What I mean is that the sound had clear—even amazingly, excitingly clear—pronunciation of syllables. M. Valdemar spoke—clearly responding to the question I had asked him just a few minutes earlier. As you'll recall, I had asked him whether he was still sleeping. He now said:

"Yes—no—I was sleeping—and now—now—I'm dead."

No one present even tried to deny or suppress the unspeakable, bone-chilling horror that these few words, spoken in this way, were perfectly designed to create. Mr. L—l (the student) fainted. The nurses immediately left the room and could not be convinced to come back. I wouldn't even attempt to make my own feelings understandable to the reader. For nearly an hour, we kept ourselves busy in silence—without saying a single word—trying to bring Mr. L—l back to consciousness. When he regained awareness, we turned our attention once again to examining M. Valdemar's condition.

Everything remained exactly as I had previously described, except that the mirror no longer showed any signs of breathing. When I tried to draw blood from his arm, the attempt was unsuccessful. I should also mention that this limb was no longer under my control. I tried unsuccessfully to make it move in the direction of my hand. The only genuine sign of the mesmeric influence was now found in the vibrating movement of his tongue whenever I asked M. Valdemar a question. He appeared to be trying to respond, but no longer had enough willpower. When anyone other than myself asked him questions, he seemed completely unaware—even though I tried to establish a mesmeric connection between him and each person in the room. I believe I have now described everything necessary to understand the sleep-walker's condition at this time. Additional nurses were brought in, and at ten o'clock I left the house with the two physicians and Mr. L——l.

In the afternoon we all visited the patient again. His condition stayed exactly the same. We discussed whether it would be appropriate and possible to wake him up, but we easily agreed that doing so wouldn't serve any useful purpose. It was clear that, up to this point, death (or what people normally call death) had been stopped by the hypnotic process. It seemed obvious to all of us that waking M. Valdemar would simply guarantee his immediate, or at least his rapid, death.

From this time until the end of last week—a period of almost seven months—we kept visiting M. Valdemar's house every day, sometimes bringing along medical colleagues and other friends. Throughout this entire time, the person who was both sleeping and awake stayed exactly as I had previously described him. The nurses provided constant care.

Last Friday, we finally decided to conduct the experiment of waking him up, or at least trying to wake him; and it's the possibly unfortunate outcome of this experiment that has sparked so much debate in private circles—so much of what I can't help but consider unjustified public sentiment.

To bring M. Valdemar out of the hypnotic trance, I used the standard hand movements. At first, these attempts failed to work. The initial sign of awakening came when his iris began to descend partially. What struck us as particularly noteworthy was that this lowering of the pupil occurred alongside a heavy discharge of yellowish fluid from under his eyelids, which gave off a sharp and extremely unpleasant smell.

It was now suggested that I should try to influence the patient's arm, as I had done before. I made the attempt and failed. Dr. F—— then indicated that he wanted me to ask a question. I did so, as follows:

"Mr. Valdemar, can you tell us what you're feeling or what you want right now?"

There was an immediate return of the feverish red circles on the cheeks; the tongue trembled, or more accurately thrashed wildly in the mouth (though the jaws and lips stayed stiff as before), and finally the same horrifying voice that I have already described burst out:

"For God's sake!—quick!—quick!—put me to sleep—or, quick!—wake me up!—quick!—I'm telling you that I am dead!"

I was completely shaken, and for a moment I couldn't decide what to do. Initially I tried to calm the patient down; but when this failed because he had completely lost control of his will, I changed course and worked just as hard to wake him up. During this attempt I quickly realized I would succeed—or at least I quickly convinced myself that my success would be total—and I'm certain that everyone in the room was ready to see the patient wake up.

For what actually happened, though, no human being could have possibly been prepared.

As I quickly performed the hypnotic gestures, while cries of "dead! dead!" erupted from the patient's tongue rather than his lips, his entire body suddenly—in the span of just one minute, or perhaps even less—withered, collapsed, and completely decomposed beneath my hands. On the bed, in front of the entire group, there remained a nearly liquid mass of disgusting and revolting decay.

The Black Cat

For the most extraordinary, yet most ordinary story I am about to write, I neither expect nor ask for belief. I would indeed be insane to expect it, in a situation where my own senses refuse to accept what they witnessed. Yet I am not insane—and I am certainly not dreaming. But tomorrow I die, and today I want to unburden my soul. My immediate goal is to present to the world, clearly, briefly, and without commentary, a series of simple domestic incidents. In their aftermath, these incidents have terrified—have tormented—have destroyed me. Yet I will not try to explain them. To me, they have shown little but horror—to many they will seem less frightening than bizarre. In the future, perhaps, some mind may be found that will reduce my nightmare to the ordinary—some mind more calm, more rational, and far less emotional than my own, which will see, in the circumstances I describe with terror, nothing more than a normal sequence of very natural causes and effects.

From childhood, I was known for being gentle and kind-hearted. My compassionate nature was so obvious that my friends often teased me about it. I had a particular love for animals, and my parents spoiled me with many different pets. I spent most of my time with these creatures and felt happiest when I was feeding them and showing them affection. This trait became stronger as I grew older, and as an adult, it became one of my greatest joys. For anyone who has loved a loyal and intelligent dog, I hardly need to explain the kind of deep satisfaction this brings. There's something about the pure, selfless love of an animal that touches the heart of someone who has often experienced the shallow friendships and fragile loyalty that humans offer.

I got married at a young age and was delighted to discover that my wife had a temperament that matched well with mine. When she noticed how much I loved household pets, she made every effort to get us the most pleasant kinds of animals. We owned birds, goldfish, a beautiful dog, rabbits, a small monkey, and a cat.

This cat was an exceptionally large and beautiful creature, completely black, and intelligent to an amazing extent. When discussing his cleverness, my wife, who deep down had a touch of superstitious belief, often referenced the old folk belief that considered all black cats to be witches in disguise. She was never actually serious about this idea— and I only bring up this detail because it happens to come to mind right now.

Pluto—that was the cat's name—was my favorite pet and companion. I was the only one who fed him, and he followed me everywhere I went around the house. It was actually hard for me to stop him from coming with me when I walked through the streets.

Our friendship continued in this way for several years, during which my overall mood and personality—through the influence of my drinking problem—had (I'm ashamed to admit) undergone a complete change for the worse. Day by day, I became more sullen, more easily angered, and more careless about other people's feelings. I allowed myself to speak harshly to my wife. Eventually, I even physically hurt her. My pets, naturally, felt the shift in my behavior. I didn't just ignore them—I mistreated them. However, I still cared enough about Pluto to stop myself from abusing him, unlike the rabbits, monkey, or even the dog, which I had no problem mistreating whenever they happened to cross my path, whether by chance or out of affection. But my condition worsened—for what illness compares to alcoholism!—and eventually even Pluto, who was getting older and therefore somewhat cranky, began to suffer from my bad temper.

One night, coming home heavily drunk from one of my usual places around town, I thought the cat was avoiding me. I grabbed him, and in his terror at my violent behavior, he bit my hand and left a small wound. The rage of a demon immediately took control of me. I no longer recognized myself. My true soul seemed to instantly leave my body, and a wickedness worse than any devil's, fed by alcohol, coursed through every part of my being. I pulled a penknife from my vest pocket, opened it, grabbed the poor animal by the throat, and intentionally cut out one of its eyes! I feel shame, I burn with guilt, I tremble with horror as I write about this terrible act.

When my rational thinking came back in the morning—after I had slept away the effects of the night's drinking—I felt a mixture of horror and guilt for the crime I had committed; but this feeling was weak and uncertain at best, and my soul remained unchanged. I threw myself back into excessive behavior, and quickly drowned all memory of what I had done in alcohol.

In the meantime the cat slowly recovered. The socket of the lost eye presented, it is true, a frightful appearance, but he no longer appeared to suffer any pain. He went about the house as usual, but, as might be expected, fled in extreme terror at my approach. I had so much of my old heart left, as to be at first grieved by this evident dislike on the part of a creature which had once so loved me. But this feeling soon gave place to irritation. And then came, as if to my final and irrevocable overthrow, the spirit of

PERVERSENESS. Of this spirit philosophy takes no account. Yet I am not more sure that my soul lives, than I am that perverseness is one of the primitive impulses of the human heart—one of the indivisible primary faculties, or sentiments, which give direction to the character of Man. Who has not, a hundred times, found himself committing a vile or a silly action, for no other reason than because he knows he should not? Have we not a perpetual inclination, in the teeth of our best judgment, to violate that which is Law, merely because we understand it to be such? This spirit of perverseness, I say, came to my final overthrow. It was this unfathomable longing of the soul to vex itself—to offer violence to its own nature—to do wrong for the wrong's sake only—that urged me to continue and finally to consummate the injury I had inflicted upon the unoffending brute. One morning, in cool blood, I slipped a noose about its neck and hung it to the limb of a tree;—hung it with the tears streaming from my eyes, and with the bitterest remorse at my heart;—hung it because I knew that it had loved me, and because I felt it had given me no reason of offence;—hung it because I knew that in so doing I was committing a sin—a deadly sin that would so jeopardize my immortal soul as to place it—if such a thing wore possible—even beyond the reach of the infinite mercy of the Most Merciful and Most Terrible God.

On the night after this terrible act was committed, I was awakened from sleep by someone shouting "Fire!" The curtains around my bed were burning. The entire house was engulfed in flames. My wife, a servant, and I barely managed to escape from the fire. Everything was destroyed. All of my possessions were consumed, and from that moment on, I gave myself over to despair.

I am beyond the weakness of trying to establish a sequence of cause and effect between the disaster and the atrocity. However, I am describing a chain of facts—and I don't want to leave even a possible connection incomplete. On the day following the fire, I visited the ruins. The walls, with one exception, had collapsed. This exception was a compartment wall, not very thick, which stood about the middle of the house, and against which the head of my bed had rested. The plaster had here, to a great extent, withstood the fire's effects—a fact which I attributed to its having been recently applied. Around this wall a dense crowd had gathered, and many people seemed to be examining a particular section of it with very close and eager attention. The words "strange!" "unusual!" and other similar expressions aroused my curiosity. I approached and saw, as if carved in bas relief upon the white surface, the figure of a gigantic cat. The impression was rendered with truly remarkable accuracy. There was a rope around the animal's neck.

When I first saw this ghostly image—because I could hardly think of it as anything else—I was filled with both amazement and fear. But eventually, logical thinking helped me understand what had happened. I recalled that the cat had been hanged in a garden next to the house. When the fire alarm sounded, this garden quickly filled with people— and one of them must have cut the animal down from the tree and hurled it through an open window into my room. This was probably done to wake me up from my sleep. When the other walls collapsed, they pressed the victim of my cruelty into the newly applied plaster; the lime in the plaster, combined with the flames and the ammonia from the dead body, had created the image I was now seeing.

Although I easily explained to my logical mind, if not completely to my conscience, the shocking event I just described, it still made a profound impact on my imagination. For months I couldn't free myself from the ghost-like image of the cat; and during this time, a feeling that resembled remorse, though it wasn't quite that, returned to my soul. I even went as far as to feel sorry about losing the animal, and I began searching around me, in the wretched places I now regularly visited, for another pet of the same kind and with a somewhat similar look to replace it.

One night as I sat there, half-dazed, in a place of terrible reputation, something black suddenly caught my eye. It was resting on top of one of the enormous barrels of gin or rum that made up most of the room's furnishings. I had been staring steadily at the top of this barrel for several minutes, and what surprised me now was that I hadn't noticed the object there sooner. I walked over to it and reached out to touch it with my hand. It was a black cat—a very large one—just as big as Pluto, and it looked exactly like him in every way except for one difference. Pluto didn't have a single white hair anywhere on his body, but this cat had a large, though irregularly shaped patch of white fur that covered almost his entire chest. The moment I touched him, he stood up immediately, purred loudly, rubbed against my hand, and seemed thrilled by my attention. This was exactly the kind of creature I had been looking for. I immediately offered to buy it from the landlord, but the man claimed no ownership of it—he knew nothing about it—had never seen it before.

I kept petting the cat, and when I got ready to head home, the animal showed that it wanted to come with me. I let it follow along, stopping now and then to give it a pat as we walked. Once we arrived at the house, it made itself completely at home right away and quickly became my wife's beloved companion.

As for me, I quickly began to feel a growing dislike for the animal. This was completely opposite to what I had expected, but for reasons I couldn't understand, its obvious affection for me actually disgusted and irritated me. Gradually, these feelings of disgust and irritation grew into bitter hatred. I started avoiding the creature, though a certain sense of shame and the memory of my previous act of cruelty kept me from physically harming it. For several weeks, I didn't hit it or mistreat it violently in any other way, but little by little—very slowly—I began to regard it with unspeakable revulsion, and I would quietly escape from its repulsive presence as if fleeing from a deadly plague.

What certainly increased my hatred of the animal was finding out, the morning after I brought it home, that like Pluto, it too had lost one of its eyes. This detail, however, only made my wife love it more, since she possessed, to a remarkable degree, that compassionate nature which had once been my defining characteristic and the foundation of many of my most innocent and genuine joys.

Despite my growing hatred for this cat, it seemed to become even more attached to me. It followed me around with a persistence that would be hard for anyone to understand. Whenever I sat down, it would crouch under my chair or jump onto my lap, smothering me with its disgusting affection. When I got up to walk, it would weave between my feet and nearly trip me, or dig its long, sharp claws into my clothing and climb up to my chest. During these moments, even though I desperately wanted to kill it with a single strike, I held myself back—partly because I remembered my previous crime, but mainly—let me admit this right now—because I was absolutely terrified of the creature.

This fear wasn't exactly a fear of physical harm—yet I would struggle to describe it any other way. I'm almost embarrassed to admit—yes, even here in this criminal's cell, I'm almost embarrassed to admit—that the terror and horror this animal filled me with had been intensified by one of the most ridiculous fantasies anyone could imagine. My wife had pointed out to me, several times, the shape of the white hair marking I've mentioned, which was the only visible difference between this strange creature and the one I had killed. The reader will recall that this mark, though large, had originally been very unclear; but gradually—so gradually it was almost unnoticeable, and for a long time my mind fought to dismiss it as imagination—it had eventually taken on a sharp, distinct outline. It now represented something that makes me tremble to mention—and because of this, more than anything else, I despised and feared the creature and would have gotten rid of the monster if I had the courage—it was now, I tell you, the image of something horrible—something ghastly—the GALLOWS!—oh, that sorrowful and terrible instrument of Horror and Crime—of Suffering and Death!

Now I was truly miserable beyond ordinary human suffering. A wild animal—whose companion I had scornfully killed—a wild animal was bringing about my downfall—me, a man created in God's image—causing me such unbearable anguish! Unfortunately, I no longer experienced the comfort of rest, either during the day or at night! During daylight hours, the creature never left me alone for a single moment, and at night I woke up every hour from nightmares of indescribable terror to discover the animal's warm breath on my face, and its enormous weight—a living nightmare that I couldn't escape—pressing down on my chest forever!

Under the weight of such torment, the weak traces of goodness left in me gave way. Dark thoughts became my only companions—the blackest and most wicked of thoughts. My naturally moody disposition grew into hatred for everything and everyone; while my long-suffering wife, sadly, bore the brunt of the sudden, frequent, and uncontrollable fits of rage that I now recklessly gave in to, enduring them with the most patience and suffering the most from them.

One day she came with me on a household task down to the cellar of the old building that our financial struggles forced us to live in. The cat followed me down the narrow stairs and nearly sent me tumbling forward, which drove me into a furious rage. I grabbed an axe, and in my anger, I forgot the childlike fear that had always prevented me from acting before. I swung at the animal with a blow that certainly would have killed it instantly if it had landed where I intended. But my wife's hand stopped the blow mid-swing. Her interference pushed me into a rage that was more than demonic, so I pulled my arm away from her grip and drove the axe deep into her skull. She collapsed and died right there on the spot, without making a sound.

After completing this terrible murder, I immediately began the careful task of hiding the body. I realized I couldn't take it out of the house during the day or at night without risking being seen by the neighbors. Numerous ideas came to mind. At one point, I considered chopping the corpse into small pieces and burning them. Then I thought about digging a grave in the cellar floor. I also considered throwing it down the well in the yard or packing it in a crate like regular goods, arranging for a delivery person to carry it away from the house. Eventually, I came up with what seemed like a much better solution than any of these options. I decided to seal it behind a wall in the cellar, just as medieval monks were known to do with their victims.

The cellar was perfectly suited for this purpose. The walls were built with loose construction and had recently been covered with rough plaster that the moist air had kept from properly setting. Additionally, one wall featured a bulge created by a blocked-off chimney or fireplace that had been sealed and designed to match the rest of the cellar. I felt confident I could easily remove the bricks at this spot, place the body inside, and rebuild the wall exactly as it was before, ensuring no one would notice anything unusual. My calculations proved correct. Using a crowbar, I quickly removed the bricks and carefully positioned the corpse against the inner wall, holding it steady while I rebuilt the entire structure to its original appearance with minimal effort. After gathering mortar, sand, and hair with extreme care, I mixed plaster that perfectly matched the existing material and meticulously covered the new brickwork. Once finished, I was completely satisfied with the result. The wall showed absolutely no signs of disturbance. I collected every piece of debris from the floor with painstaking attention to detail. Looking around with a sense of triumph, I told myself: "Here at least, then, my labor has not been in vain."

My next step was to search for the animal that had caused so much misery; I had finally made a firm decision to kill it. If I had been able to find it at that moment, there would have been no question about what would happen to it; but it seemed that the cunning creature had been frightened by the intensity of my earlier rage, and chose not to show itself while I was in this state of mind. It's impossible to describe or even imagine the profound, wonderful sense of relief that the absence of this hated animal brought to my heart. It didn't appear during the night; and so for one night at least, since it had been brought into the house, I slept deeply and peacefully; yes, I slept even with the weight of murder on my conscience!

The second and third days went by, and my tormentor still hadn't appeared. Once more, I could breathe like a free man. The creature had fled the house forever in fear! I would never see it again! My joy was overwhelming! The guilt from my terrible act barely bothered me. A few questions had been asked, but I had easily answered them. They had even conducted a search—but naturally, nothing could be found. I considered my future happiness guaranteed.

On the fourth day after the murder, a group of police officers arrived at the house completely without warning and began conducting another thorough search of the property. However, confident in the perfect secrecy of my hiding place, I felt absolutely no anxiety. The officers asked me to join them during their investigation. They examined every single corner and crevice. Eventually, for the third or fourth time, they went down into the cellar. I didn't tremble even slightly. My heart remained as steady as someone sleeping peacefully with a clear conscience. I strolled through the cellar from one end to the other. I crossed my arms over my chest and wandered back and forth with complete ease. The police were completely satisfied with their search and got ready to leave. The joy in my heart was too overwhelming to contain. I felt compelled to say just one thing as a victory statement, something that would make their certainty of my innocence absolutely unshakeable.

"Gentlemen," I finally said as the group climbed the stairs, "I'm delighted to have put your suspicions to rest. I wish you all good health, and perhaps a bit more politeness. By the way, gentlemen, this—this is a very well-built house." (In my desperate need to say something casually, I barely knew what words were coming out of my mouth.)—"I can honestly say it's an excellently well-built house. These walls—are you leaving, gentlemen?—these walls are solidly constructed;" and here, driven by pure reckless boldness, I struck hard with a walking stick I carried in my hand against that exact section of brickwork behind which lay the dead body of my beloved wife.

But may God protect and save me from the claws of the Devil! As soon as the echo of my strikes faded into silence, a voice from inside the tomb answered me!—a cry that began muffled and fragmented, like a child's weeping, then rapidly grew into one long, loud, and unending scream, completely unnatural and inhuman—a howl—a wailing shriek that was half terror and half victory, the kind that could only emerge from hell itself, rising together from the throats of the damned in their torment and the demons who rejoice in their destruction.

It would be pointless to describe my own thoughts at that moment. Feeling faint, I stumbled backward against the opposite wall. For a brief moment, the group on the stairs stood completely still, paralyzed by extreme terror and shock. The next instant, a dozen strong arms were working frantically at the wall. It collapsed entirely. The corpse, already severely decomposed and covered with dried blood, stood upright before the horrified onlookers. On its head, with its red gaping mouth and single glowing eye, perched the terrible creature whose cunning had led me to commit murder, and whose betraying cry had sealed my fate with the executioner. I had sealed the monster inside the tomb with me!

THE END

Thank You For Reading

You've Just Read a Piece of the Greatest Library Ever Rebuilt

Thank you for reading.

This book is one of thousands we're restoring, reimagining, and translating as part of the **Modern Library of Alexandria** — a global movement to preserve and share humanity's most important ideas.

What was once lost to fire and time is now rising again — not just as memory, but as living, breathing knowledge, freely accessible to all.

What You Can Do Next:

*   **Keep Reading.**

    Discover more legendary works — in beautiful print, audiobook, or digital form — at LibraryofAlexandria.com.

*   **Build Your Own Library.**

    Every title is available as a paperback, hardcover, or collectible boxset — at true printing cost. Craft a personal library worthy of display.

*   **Spread the Light.**

    Share this book. Tell others about the movement. Help us translate every timeless work into every language, so no reader is ever left behind.

By finishing this book, you've already taken part in something extraordinary.

Join us at LibraryofAlexandria.com

Together, we're rebuilding the greatest library the world has ever known.

With appreciation,

The Modern Library of Alexandria Team

Visit:
www.libraryofalexandria.com
Or scan the code below: